Power of Workbooking

Taking time to workbook is a powerful act of self-care. Did you know that setting time aside each day to connect with yourself is a powerful way to help you gain self-awareness? Without self-awareness, it is nearly impossible to create change.

Over the next 30 days, I encourage you to schedule a time each day where you will allow yourself the time and space to sit in a peaceful environment so you can fulfill this journey. The suggested daily time is a minimum of 15-30 minutes, as this time is sufficient to work on the exercises you will be introduced to. By daily Workbooking, you will begin to feel more centered, gain clarity, and experience more connection.

Take your time through this experience and remember you can come back to this practice at any time, even after you complete the Workbook and Guide. And please remember, there are no right or wrong answers. This is YOUR experience.

Commitment Note

I _____, am committed to using my Workbook as a guide to empower me as I work towards reaching my highest potential. I will allow myself a minimum of 15-30 minutes a day to work on the exercises provided in this Workbook. I will especially remember to create a safe, calm environment where I can allow myself to be vulnerable and present throughout this experience.

I thank myself for taking the time to do this work.

_____

(Sign your name and put today's date)

Hi Beautiful! Now that you have signed your Commitment Note, I encourage you to take this page out of the Workbook and Guide and hang it in a place you can see daily. Maybe you will pin it to the fridge, on your bathroom mirror, or maybe you will carry it in your purse. Whatever you choose to do, stay committed to you.

-SC

Mindfulness
Defined

About this Experience

Mindful Makeover is a Workbook and Guide for women who are ready to begin creating the life they desire. Mindful Makeover has been created to take you on a 30-day journey that will allow you to experience a complete MAKEOVER. By the end of this experience, you will have learned how to live Mindfully, be a deliberate thinker, and you will be aligned with your true essence and most authentic self.

Within this Workbook and Guide, you are offered evidence-based and thought-provoking questions, inspirational quotes written by the author, and education on neuroscience, otherwise known as behavioral psychology. Every question has been designed to help you obtain and embrace the following: Awareness, Acceptance, Accountability, and Action. Get excited as you begin the journey of achieving a Mindful Makeover.

Table of Contents

Introduction

Hello Beautiful and welcome to Mindful Makeover! Congratulations on making yourself a priority. By making this commitment you have sent a message to the universe that you are ready and willing to begin creating the life you desire.

I am so excited that you have made the decision to go on this 30-day journey. You are worthy and deserving of living the life you desire and I am so thankful you chose Mindful Makeover as your guide. Throughout my career, I have worked with thousands of individuals and nothing makes me feel more alive than to be a witness to a person's individualized transformation and growth. It is an incredible feeling when we realize everything we need lives inside of us and we are powerful beings beyond measure. You have the ability to create the life you desire simply by using your own thoughts.

I can remember a time in my life when I was living on "auto-pilot." I would wake up, go through the everyday motions, just to go to sleep, wake up and repeat it all. I had no internal or external awareness. I can remember questioning my meaning and purpose, feeling lost and confused, with no idea where to even begin. While sure, I thought I was happy, I also questioned "am I really happy?" Then one day, the light bulb was turned on.

I can remember vividly feeling like there must be more to life. I started to explore who I was as an individual. I wanted to get to know myself beyond my name and the things I was a part of. I evaluated the people, places, and things I was associated with and began to read self-help books, do research, and google anything and everything that came to mind about living life to the fullest. Sounds crazy, right? During this time of my life, I was also in graduate school working on my Master of Social Work. Through my own search and education, I was introduced to many practices, but the one that really resonated with me was Mindfulness.

The moment I learned of Mindfulness and the benefits I was determined to teach others. I did extensive research on this practice, and attended several workshops and groups on Mindfulness. I have included Mindfulness as a daily activity for the past five years in my own life. I believe strongly in this practice and I am passionate about it because I have not only witnessed the direct benefits, but also, because it is my belief that this practice is the doorway to creating a desirable life. It allows a person to be present and to experience life to the fullest. My passion and determination are what led me to write Mindful Makeover. I hope you find this Workbook and Guide to be simple, yet challenging. Take your time and embrace this experience.

Stephanie's Education & Credentials

Stephanie Catalano is a licensed mental health professional with the state of Florida, life coach, motivational speaker, and writer. She earned her Bachelor of Science in Sociology and her Master of Social Work. She is also the published author of *Bonafide Spirit* and *Painted Soul*. Stephanie's career experience is in child welfare, mental health, and substance use disorders.

Mindfulness, a practice that can truly change your life dramatically.

I'm sure most of you have heard of this practice and maybe you have even attempted to live by it. However, it is something that is hard to remain dedicated to due to the pace of everyday life. Mindfulness is really an activity. It's something that needs to be practiced daily so it can become a "state of mind." It's one thing to read a book or attend an inspiring workshop, but it's entirely different when it comes to actually designing a life that allows you to live mindfully, be a deliberate thinker, and align with your true essence and most authentic self.

Mindfulness has been defined in many ways, but in essence, mindfulness is a psychological process of bringing one's attention to experiences occurring in the present moment. This practice assists you in being able to remain open and active to what is going on in each moment, as well as to remain present without passing judgment.

To be mindful is to allow yourself to observe your thoughts and feelings without judging them as "positive" or "negative." It is also to live life in the moment rather than watching your life pass you by or "waiting for the right moment." To be mindful also means to experience life as it's happening rather than dwelling on your past or worrying about your future.

Benefits of Mindfulness

- Stress reduction
- Boosts to working memory
- Increases focus
- Less emotional reactivity
- More cognitive flexibility
- Improves relationships

- Decreases anxiety
- Increases immune functioning
- Overall improvement of well-being
- Enhances mental health
- Increases emotional regulation and self-control

Attitudes Of
Mindfulness

Here are the seven attitudes of mindfulness according to Jon Kabat-Zinn.
(Kabat-Zinn, 2004, p. 32)

No Judgment - allow yourself to live in each moment, without passing judgment.
Become the observer of your experience.

Non-Striving - there is no goal other than to be your authentic self and live life honoring your true essence.
It is about feeling happy and fulfilled. It is knowing that you deserve to experience bliss and you are
capable of creating the life you desire.

Acceptance - this is a willingness to not only see things as they are, but also to accept what is. This is especially
important regarding matters outside of you, that you have no control over. Accept each passing moment for what
it is. This allows you to experience everything life has to offer and learn along the way.

Letting Go - don't hold onto anything that doesn't support your highest and best self. This includes thoughts,
feelings, ideas, your past. And all the "should of, could of, would of." Letting go requires you to not be consumed
with attachments you have. It also means if and when you experience rejection, it's okay. Let it go. Move on.
People, places, things, and situations don't define you. You are more than that! When experiencing a negative
thought or unpleasant feeling, allow yourself the time and space to process the feeling, letting it flow
through you and out of you.

Beginner's Mind - this is really about allowing yourself to start over. To start fresh without having any
expectations. Remove the attachment from the past and allow yourself to be open. Having a beginner's mind is to
let go of your own agenda, and experience the moments as they pass by. It's important you remain present.

Patience - this is to remember things happen when they are supposed to. Having patience is an important part of
Mindfulness, for it allows you to stay present without experiencing unnecessary anxiety, fear, panic, or worry.

Trust - it's important to trust yourself and the process. It's also important that you give yourself permission
to trust your feelings. Allow yourself to feel confident, knowing everything is working out for you.

The Magic Four

Awareness + Acceptance + Accountability + Action = Mindful Makeover

Within this Workbook and Guide you will be offered 30 questions that take you through The Magic Four: Awareness, Acceptance, Accountability, and Action. The Magic Four is the roadmap that leads you to achieve a Mindful Makeover.

Awareness

Awareness of self has been defined as "conscious knowledge of one's own character, feelings, motives, and desires."

Having self-awareness is important because it is this that allows an individual to have a clear understanding of their strengths, weaknesses, thoughts, beliefs, emotions, and it also helps discover your why.

Self-awareness also allows you to understand how other people perceive you, your outlook on people, places, and things, as well as the reason you react and respond to certain people and situations.

In order to become aware, you must spend time exploring yourself and your experiences as a way to identify the root of how you perceive and understand all that you experience.

Having self-awareness also allows for increased self-esteem and self-confidence. In order to create the life you desire, it's important to know and understand yourself. Self-awareness is the power that leads you to creating (acting).

Acceptance

Acceptance is to recognize a process or condition without attempting to change it. It is to accept something for what it is, without trying to control or change the outcome.

Acceptance of self has been defined as "an individual's satisfaction or happiness with oneself, and is thought to be necessary for good mental health." - Shepard

Self-Acceptance involves self-understanding, a realistic, subjective awareness of one's strengths and weaknesses.

When we accept what has been, what is, and what we can control versus what we can't control, we begin to experience the magic of a Mindful Makeover.

Accountability

Accountability has been defined as "the fact or condition of being accountable; otherwise referred to as responsibility."

To be accountable means to take ownership for something within one's power or control. It is to answer to your own mistakes and own them, without placing the blame on a person, place, or thing.

Holding yourself accountable saves time and energy and eliminates any chance for negative behavior.

Action

Action has been defined as the process of doing something, typically to achieve something one is aiming for.

When an individual is putting into action the skills they have learned along the way, it assists them in staying in alignment and maintaining a balanced life of mind, body, and spirit connection.

This is the most important step, however, it's nearly impossible to maintain without having awareness, acceptance, and accountability.

By now, you have been well introduced to what Mindfulness is, the attitudes of Mindfulness, and the benefits. You also have an understanding of The Magic Four. Now, it's time to begin answering the questions that have been designed to guide you through the experience of achieving a Mindful Makeover, starting with the first section on Awareness. I encourage you to allow yourself to sit in a comfortable, peaceful place. Give yourself at least 15-30 minutes a day to answer the questions you will be introduced to in the next pages. Most importantly, remember, this is YOUR experience. There is no right or wrong answer, so please be gentle with yourself and do not pass judgment on any of your thoughts, feelings, or answers.

-SC

Day 1   Awareness

This section includes questions 1-14. Please remember, the questions have been designed to introduce you to ways to gain awareness. These questions are not the only ways to gain awareness, but rather a guide to help you begin this journey.

In order to become aware, you must spend time exploring your thoughts, feelings, behaviors, and day-to-day experiences as a way to identify the root of how you understand and perceive yourself, others, and your experiences. Here are three questions to help you begin the journey of gaining self-awareness:

1. What are the two barriers that are keeping you from living in the present moment?

2. What unpleasant feelings do you most often experience? Identify at least two feelings.
   List your understanding of the root of these feelings. Where do they stem from?

   > afraid, aggravated, angry, ambivalent, alienated, agitated, ashamed, anxiety, bitter, bored, cranky, distressed, distraught, dread, displeased, disgusted, disconnected, devastated, edgy, fidgety, fearful, frustrated, gloomy, guilty, grief, helpless, heartbroken, insecure, inadequate, jealous, lonely, melancholy, mistrustful, numb, nostalgic, outraged, panicked, self-conscious, troubled, unhappy

3. What two challenges and/or problems do you feel continuously show up in your day-to-day life?
   Identify at least two challenges and/or problems:

4. Who are you? Think about what your values are to help respond to this question.

Self-awareness is one of the most beautiful gifts you can give yourself.
Dig deeper. Get to know and understand more.
- SC

1

2

3

4

Day 2

On this day, you are introduced to the power of energy and how thoughts and feelings manifest.
Manifest is a word used to indicate when thoughts becomes real. This is really important for you to understand, so here's an example:

Have you ever woken up feeling tired and run down and all you did was think about how tired and run down you felt? I bet the outcome was you continued to feel tired and run down. How can you expect to feel energized and ready for the day when you only think about how tired and run down you are? That doesn't even make sense. On the other hand, if you wake up feeling tired and run down, but you make a deliberate choice to think, "I am energized and I am ready for the day," you will manifest or make real the feeling of energized. Does this practice make sense?

Here are three questions to help you become aware of what you feed energy to the most:

1. What do you feed your energy to the most? Is it your relationship, your children, your job, the unpleasant feelings you've been experiencing?

2. In question #1 you were asked to answer what you feed your energy to the most. Now, you are invited to answer what actually drains your energy the most. For example, is your energy drained because you're always rushing, on the go? Or, do you not have anytime to do housework during the week, so your weekends are tied up with chores? Is there an individual who is reaching out to you to negatively vent or complain? Please elaborate on what your situations are and explore solutions that will help you be more Mindful as to how and where you spend your energy.

3. What role do you play in the things that drain you? In other words, how do you contribute to situations that drain you? For example, does talking to that one person drain you, yet you continue to talk to that person? Identify at least one example.

How beautiful it is to know with one single thought you can change the way you feel and the direction of your day.
The more you become self-aware, the more you will realize the power that's inside of you.
Not everyone is deserving of your energy and that's okay. Be selective.
-SC

♥ ♥ ♥

① _____
_____
_____
_____
_____
_____

② _____
_____
_____
_____
_____
_____

③ _____
_____
_____
_____
_____

Day 3

In this exercise, you will be provided with education and information about "core beliefs." Please take the time to read the facts below as this knowledge is an important part as you gain your own awareness. You aren't required to answer anything during this exercise as it's simply informative.

Core beliefs are thoughts and assumptions that are based on choices and decisions we make in life that are long forgotten and invisible to our awareness. It's important to become aware of your core beliefs as it is these beliefs that guide your behavior and determine how you view yourself, other people, and the world. Core beliefs are like boxes that people live in and become used to and this keeps people from experiencing life as it is. Core beliefs can become like walls that keep people from experiencing new possibilities and opportunities in life.

Core beliefs are nothing more than thoughts that are affirmed over and over eventually becoming a belief (For example, if a person thinks every day, "I'm not good enough," eventually they will believe that to be true). Beliefs begin in childhood and carry over into adulthood, inevitably dictating the way a person reacts or responds to all relationships and situations.

Whether you are aware of it or not, you are always affirming what you believe based on what you think. Often times, people struggle with letting their core beliefs go because the beliefs become a basis of identity. To not have a core belief could leave a person feeling as if they are nothing or questioning who they are. You didn't come into this world with a belief system, all beliefs are formed out of experiences, and given the nature of the experience, the beliefs you formed were the ones that made sense to you. The beauty is it is possible to create new core beliefs by using your thoughts.

That was a lot to take in, so I invite you to do a quick deep breathing exercise to release any overwhelming feelings and create space for a clear mind as you continue this Workbook and Guide. **Ready?**

 Sit in an upright position.
Place your hands on your thighs with your palms upward.
Keep your spine straight.
Close your eyes.

Now, breathe in.
Count down in your head: 10, 9, 8, 7, 6, 5, 4, 3, 2, 1
Exhale. Let it all out.
Repeat three times.

Deep breathing is a great practice. It's easy and has many benefits.
Keep this skill with you in your "purse."
- SC

Day 4

In this exercise you will have an opportunity to identify what your core beliefs are. Below is a list of negative and positive examples. Please circle the ones you relate to. If needed, please add to the list. This exercise doesn't require you to do anything other than identify what core beliefs you have.

Beliefs About Yourself

I don't deserve love.
I'm not good enough.
I'm a failure.
I'm a good person.
I'm worth it.
I'm smart.

_____

_____

_____

Beliefs About Relationships

I'll never be in a relationship.
I can't live without a partner.
No one ever understands me.
I can trust people.
I easily make new friends.
I am my own person even in a relationship.

_____

_____

_____

Beliefs About Life

Life is hard.
Life is unfair.
Everyone is out to get me.
Life will be what I make it.
The world is filled with good people.
There is beauty where I choose to see it.

_____

_____

_____

Appreciate all that you are and allow yourself to get excited, really excited, for who you are becoming. Regardless of what core beliefs you have, you are more than them. It's important to know no one or nothing can pronounce you enough or not enough. Only you can and it starts with your thoughts. Thoughts become beliefs. Think beautifully.

- SC

Day 5

Yesterday, on Day 4, you identified the core beliefs you have about yourself, relationships, and life. Today, I invite you to pick two of the negative core beliefs from yesterday and create a healthier, more adaptive belief. Remember, beliefs are simply thoughts that are repeatedly thought, which leads to a belief.

Here is an example:

Old belief: I don't deserve love.

New belief: I am worthy and deserving of love.

1.

Old Belief: _____

New Belief: _____

2.

Old Belief: _____

New Belief: _____

You will find it easier to think the negative beliefs more than the positive ones. That's okay and it's normal. All I ask is that when you find yourself stuck on the negative beliefs, remind yourself if you continue to think the core beliefs that don't support your highest and best self, it will be incredibly difficult to ever live the life you desire or stay aligned with your true essence and most authentic self. On the contrary, if you begin thinking and believing the core beliefs such as, "I am worthy and deserving of love," it will be incredibly easy to live the life you desire and stay aligned with your true essence and most authentic self. It takes time to create new beliefs. Be gentle. Be kind. Be loving. Be patient. This is a journey.

- SC

Day 6

In this exercise, you will create at least five affirmations that you can begin affirming daily.
To affirm is to declare something true and it also provides support. By using daily affirmations,
you will begin to rewire the way you think about and set your days up for success.
This practice will also help eliminate old core beliefs and increase your self-esteem.

Starting today, I affirm the following:

1. _____

2. _____

3. _____

4. _____

5. _____

Whatever you want, imagine it, then affirm it! Shout it out to the universe loud and proud.
When you think good, you feel good, and when you feel good, you do good!
- SC

Day 7

Have you ever felt like you're living life on autopilot? You find yourself feeling anxious, stressed, and worried. You are existing, without really living. You don't know who you are because you're constantly on the go and never have "me time." You're not sure why or how to control these feelings.

It's important to check in with yourself on a regular, consistent basis and ask, "How am I feeling today?" Although you may not always be able to control your feelings, you are responsible for how you choose to respond to your feelings. For instance, if you suddenly begin to feel anxious rather than getting into a panic, you can choose to go on a walk, read a book, practice deep breathing, or use some other skill that will help decrease the anxiety symptoms.

In this exercise, you are invited to ask yourself how do you feel most of the days? Are you content, are you stressed, are you overwhelmed?

I most often feel: _____

_____

_____

_____

Now, you are invited to write down how you would like to feel.

I would like to feel: _____

_____

_____

_____

Mantras are statements that are repeated frequently. They are used to help raise the vibration of your being.
You are invited to begin each morning with the following (or create your own mantra):
"Today, I will be happy and I will feel good no matter what is happening to me or around me."
Remember, you aren't given a good day or a bad day, you are given a day and it is your responsibility
to create the day you want. Yes, there will be things that you have to do even when you don't want to and yes, there will be
things that happen that are out of your control, but with every moment, you can choose how you want to respond.
And, when things aren't going as well as you'd like, you can stop, and change the direction of your day.
- SC

Day 8

In this exercise, I invite you to really think about whether you are held back by fear or living in the light of love. You might be wondering what I mean by this and here is what I mean. Do you find yourself not pursuing your dreams or taking steps of action towards your goals out of fear of failure or the unknown? Or, are you living in the light of love, trusting that everything will work out for you and even when things don't go as planned, the light of love still surrounds you and protects you?

I encourage you to be specific in regards to how fear and love show up in your life. Living in fear is common for most and often produced by one's own thoughts and to live in the light of love is beautiful and that's what you deserve.

1. In what ways has fear held you back? Identify at least two ways:

2. What are two changes you can make today to begin overcoming your fears?

3. How can living in the light of love help you? Identify at least two ways:

Why let fear hold you back when you can let love help you fly?
- SC

♥ ♥ ♥

① _____
_____
_____
_____
_____
_____

② _____
_____
_____
_____
_____
_____

③ _____
_____
_____
_____
_____

Day 9

To be deliberate means to carefully talk or think something through. It also means to stop, think, then respond. Being deliberate helps in making healthy decisions and conscious, thought-out choices.

1. Do you consider yourself a deliberate thinker? Explain why or why not:

2. What decisions do you most often struggle with making? Identify at least two:

3. What are two ways you can be more deliberate in your thinking?

By making decisions, it alleviates the unnecessary anxiety, stress, worry and other unpleasant feelings that one experiences from delaying decision making. When you feel unsure of what to do, follow your gut. Your intuition is usually always right. Aim to make the decision that feels "good enough" for that moment. It doesn't have to be the best decision. In fact, I'm not sure such a thing exists. After all, life is about experiencing moment after moment. Also, keeping in mind, you have the power to change your mind and make a new decision at any point. The key is making the decision. Take the chance. Be deliberate. Give yourself the time to think things through. There will never be the "right time." All you have is now.

- SC

① _____
_____
_____
_____
_____
_____

② _____
_____
_____
_____
_____
_____

③ _____
_____
_____
_____
_____
_____

Day 10

Intention Versus Attention.

Intentions are what we aim to do or plan to do. When you have an intention, it's important that you are focusing your attention only on that which supports your intention. For example, if your intention is to feel good, yet you focus on all the things that are going wrong, how can you expect to manifest your intention of feeling good? In other words, you must focus on things that make you feel good, so your desired feeling manifests. Intention and attention must be aligned. This is super important!

Use the space below to create three intentions. Be sure to also include what you will place your attention on to allow your intention to manifest.

1. My intention is: _____

_____

I will focus my attention on: _____

_____

2. My intention is: _____

_____

I will focus my attention on: _____

_____

3. My intention is: _____

_____

I will focus my attention on: _____

_____

Let this day be the kick start to your journey of using intention setting daily to create the life you desire. This is part of living a mindful life. By being clear on what it is that you want, you send a message to the universe, and naturally the universe does its wonderful magic of allowing your desires to manifest. Yes, you have to do your part and remember, things work out how they are meant to. It might not happen your way or at the time you want it to, but it absolutely will work out. It always does.

Be patient, embrace the journey, and keep living in the light of love.

After all, you are love and you are loved.

- SC

Day 11

Self-care is a beautiful way to show self-love. In order to be aligned with your true essence and most authentic self, it's important to give yourself permission to do whatever you love most and whatever makes you feel the best. This can include taking a hot bath, getting a massage, getting your nails done, or even having a day where you do nothing but stay in your jammies and watch movies.

1. In what ways do you practice self-care? Identify at least three ways:

_____

_____

_____

_____

_____

2. How can you cultivate more self-love? Identify at least three ways:

_____

_____

_____

_____

_____

No matter how busy the days are, stay committed to practicing self-care and self-love. This can be as easy as hugging yourself and saying, "I did a really good job today." It's so easy doing it for other people and I know it can be hard to make yourself a priority, especially if you have children. It might feel selfish when you put yourself first, but it's not selfish. It's a beautiful act of self-love.

- SC

Day 12

Okay, today, let's have some real talk. Women are the most powerful beings ever created. Can I get a "hell yes?" Come on. Shout it out loud! Women take on so many roles and we are really good at it. It's easy to lose yourself along the way. In this exercise, I want you to think about a time when you pretended to be okay, but deep down, you felt lost and confused. You felt unfulfilled and unhappy. Maybe, you even felt unappreciated. Whatever you felt or still feel, think about how you held back from speaking your truth to either your family, your friends, your partner (boyfriend, husband, girlfriend, wife, anyone intimate to you), your work relationships, and/or yourself.

Or maybe you're at a place in your life where you are speaking your truth and you have the confidence to always show up in the light of truth. Regardless where you are in your journey when it comes to speaking your truth, I invite you to write down an example of how you are either living in conflict with your true self or living aligned with your true self.

1. I have been living in conflict with my true self and I know this because:

_____

_____

_____

_____

_____

2. I have been living aligned with my true self and I know this because:

_____

_____

_____

_____

_____

No matter how hard it might be and even if it might create conflict, always speak your truth. Be brave and be courageous.
You are not responsible for other people's feelings and/or their reactions.
Only your own. Speak your truth and do it with love.

- SC

Day 13

In this exercise, you are invited to explore the things you are still feeding energy to from your past that no longer serve your highest and best self. Maybe you're still experiencing guilt from something you did a year ago, maybe you are holding onto shame-based beliefs about yourself, maybe you're still losing sleep over what your boss said about your performance. Whatever it is, use this space to journal about the things you need to stop feeding energy to. Once you spend time journaling, you are invited to write out at least three new things you will feed your energy to; things that support your highest and best self.

1. I am deliberately choosing to let go of:

_____

_____

_____

_____

_____

2. Starting today, I will be deliberate in feeding energy to only that which supports my highest and best self. I am doing this because I know by feeding energy to positive things that will help me grow and evolve as a person.

1. _____

_____

2. _____

_____

3. _____

_____

Give yourself permission to dissolve your
past. It deserves to rest.
All that matters is now. ACTIVATE
the present moment.
- SC

Day 14

In this exercise, you will answer questions that are designed to help you better understand yourself.
Allow this space to really think about who you are and what it is that you truly desire. You are more than your name,
you are more than your weight, you are more than your career, you are more than your education, and you are
more than the roles you have. There are no rules or limits. You can be and you can have whatever it is you want.
You are also encouraged to be vulnerable and make an honest assessment about yourself.

1. What are your some of your achievements, strengths and weaknesses?

2. What motivates you and makes you feel your best?

3. What would you like to improve as a person?

Hi Beautiful! Congratulations! At this point of the Workbook and Guide, you've done so much work
on yourself and you have completed the section on awareness. How does it feel to have more knowledge
and a better understanding of yourself? You are aware of your thoughts and feelings and you understand
the power of each thought. You know your strengths and you aren't afraid of your weaknesses.
You are acknowledging your successes and you are showing up through the light of love and your truth.
You are honoring your true essence and most authentic self. Now, let's begin the second part
of The Magic Four: Acceptance.

Be true to you and authentic in all you do.
- SC

1

2

3

Day 15   Acceptance

This section includes questions 15-20. Please remember, the questions have been designed to introduce you to ways to work towards acceptance. These questions are not the only ways to achieve acceptance, but rather a guide to help you begin this journey.

In this exercise, you will use your own words to define acceptance, courage, and wisdom.

1. To me acceptance is: _____

_____

_____

_____

2. To me courage is: _____

_____

_____

_____

3. To me wisdom is: _____

_____

_____

_____

The "Serenity Prayer" is a prayer I use daily. It's beautiful and a helpful reminder, so I want to share it with you:
"God grant me the serenity to ACCEPT the things I cannot change, the COURAGE to change the things I can,
and the WISDOM to know the difference." If this resonates with you, I encourage you use this prayer as often as needed.
- SC

Day 16

In this exercise, I invite you to write out what it is you have to accept, what it is you need to have courage for, and how you can have the wisdom to know the difference of what you can and cannot change.

1. I accept: _____

_____

_____

_____

2. I have the courage to: _____

_____

_____

_____

3. I am wise enough to: _____

_____

_____

_____

Live as if and always expect the best. When we live as if we already have and have done the things we need to do, it allows us to feel good. Living as if everything is working out for you will raise your vibration. All this really means is you will vibrate at a higher frequency, which makes it easier to create and attract all that you desire.
- SC

Day 17

Part of acceptance is letting go of blame and resentments. In order to truly experience a Mindful Makeover, it's important to identify who or what you're blaming and what resentments you're carrying with you. Blame and Resentments aren't accessories. Let it go. Blame is to "assign responsibility for a fault or wrong," whereas resentment is "bitter indignation at having been treated unfairly." Letting go of blame and resentment is a really big step. This is the step that can truly set you free. Take a deep breath and remember this is your experience. Complete this exercise at a pace that feels good to you.

1. Today, I am choosing to be deliberate in letting go of the following blame and resentments
   I have been carrying, for I know this will set me free:

_____

_____

_____

_____

_____

_____

_____

_____

It can be really difficult to let go of blame and resentment, especially when you have been hurt by someone.
But, please take this in: the moment you let go, and I mean really let it go by releasing the feelings that come with blame
and resentment, you will be set free. You deserve to be free. Holding onto blame and resentment is like punishing yourself.
Think about it. The person who hurt you isn't suffering over what they did to you. Only you suffer by holding onto it.
A lot of times, people get stuck in a place of blame and resentment because they don't want to feel what's under
the wound that was caused by whoever hurt them. It's easier to place blame and stay resentful because that distracts
the person from feeling their wounds. But, it's okay to feel. To feel is to heal and to heal is to feel.
- SC

43

Day 18

In this exercise, you are invited to write out what is in your control versus what you can't control. Identify at least five things each. Although it can be difficult to accept certain things that aren't in your control, it's important to have this understanding so that you can create the life you desire. Often times, women end up trying to control everything, which only delays the flow of attracting desires.

What's in my control: _____

_____

_____

_____

_____

_____

What's not in my control: _____

_____

_____

_____

_____

_____

You don't have the power to control everything, but you are powerful. Every human wants to be in control.
It's part of the human nature. Once you realize you have the power to control your thoughts,
how you feel or respond to your feelings, and how you respond to the outside world, it truly is life changing.
- SC

Day 19

In this exercise, you are invited to identify the biggest thing you are willing to accept. I say the "biggest thing" because I want you to think about whatever it is that has become a barrier to you living in the present moment because you are struggling to accept what is. Take your time thinking about this. Once you decide to accept something, whether it be a person or situation, it will relieve the unpleasant feeling(s) you have been experiencing.

1. What is it that you're willing to accept? _____

_____

_____

_____

_____

_____

2. What are three things you can do to help you through the process of accepting this person or situation?

_____

_____

_____

Freedom is to accept what is and to release all that you can't control.

- SC

Day 20

In this exercise, you are encouraged to write an acceptance letter to yourself. If you are not in the space of readiness to write an acceptance letter to yourself, then you are encouraged to write a peace letter to your past. The purpose of this exercise is to accept who you are and know your self-worth, regardless of what your past has been. When we accept the things that are outside of our control, including our past, it truly is the doorway to freedom. By accepting what is, it creates space to allow yourself to begin creating the life you desire, while staying aligned with your true essence and most authentic self. It also allows you to begin living in the present because you have accepted whatever has been interfering with your ability to live in the present. You are always welcomed to come back to this exercise when you feel ready.

Dear Self:

or

Dear Past:

Hi Beautiful! Congratulations! At this point of the Workbook and Guide, you've done so much work on yourself and you have completed the section on acceptance. How does it feel to have accepted what is and to have let go of what you can't control? You are working hard to stay focused on only the things you have control over and you are beginning to realize how powerful you are. You are no longer carrying blame and resentment. You are able to let things go quickly, which has allowed you to be more present for the days. Now, let's begin the third part of The Magic Four: Accountability.

True beauty is in the raw moments where you accept yourself during the successes and the struggles.
During the wins and the losses. During the moments where you feel like you are soaring high
and the moments where you feel like you're crashing down, accept yourself.
There is only one of you and there is something really special knowing that.
- SC

Dear Self

_____

_____

_____

_____

_____

_____

_____

_____

_____

_____

Dear Past

_____

_____

_____

_____

_____

_____

_____

_____

_____

Day 21   Accountability

This section includes questions 21-25. Please remember, the questions have been designed to introduce you to ways to work towards taking accountability. These questions are not the only ways to help you become accountable, but rather a guide to help you fulfill this journey.

Did you know people often blame people and things for their own actions as a way to not have to take accountability? Research shows people often fear accountability because with being held accountable, comes vulnerability. But you see, accountability is one of the Magic Four that creates POWER. It's far more powerful to own your choices and even mistakes than it is to blame someone or something external of you.

In this exercise, you are invited to list three ways you can be held accountable. Maybe you need be held accountable in terms of eating healthier, exercising more, or limiting your alcohol intake. This can include identifying a loved one as your "accountability partner."

I will hold myself accountable by doing the following:

1. _____

2. _____

3. _____

Your reality is a direct result of your thoughts. No one can create your reality
except you and it's your responsibility to create the life you desire.
It is a waste of time and energy blaming people and things
and it is a powerful force when accountability is taken.
-SC

Day 22

In this exercise, you are invited to visualize the perfect day, from your perspective. Often times, people are rushing, leaving themselves with little to no time to do the things that they most enjoy. Here are three questions to help you begin thinking and visualizing your perfect day.

1. Use the space below to write out what your perfect day looks like:

_____

_____

_____

_____

2. What do you feel when you allow yourself to imagine your perfect day? Do you feel happy and at peace, do you feel fun and silly, are you filled with love and laughter?

_____

_____

_____

_____

3. What are three things you can do, starting today, to begin creating days that look more like your perfect day?

_____

_____

_____

_____

The best thing about a perfect day is you get to define your perfect.
Make every day the best day!
- SC

Day 23

Yesterday, you visualized your perfect day. Today, you will identify at least three triggers/stressors that become barriers to you experiencing the day you wrote about yesterday. The intent of this exercise is not only to recognize what gets in the way of your days, but also to take accountability by owning your part in how you respond to triggers/stressors and work towards creating a new perspective.

Example: Trigger/Stressor: Stress

Old perspective:

Everything in my life is stressful. I am tired of doing so much just to be left feeling stressed.

New perspective:

I have a lot of responsibilities, but I am going to begin practicing self-care.
I know self-care will help relieve my stress.

Trigger/Stressor:

Old perspective: _____

_____

New perspective: _____

_____

It is really difficult to create new perspectives and break free from conditioned responses otherwise
known as automatic responses. Responses are learned throughout life and inevitably the brain becomes programmed
to respond certain ways to certain stimuli associated with triggers/stressors. The good news is, it is absolutely possible
to create new perspectives and break free from conditioned responses. However, it does require consistent effort and hard work.
When you find yourself struggling with old perspectives and conditioned responses, here is one skill you can practice:
Stop, acknowledge that you're experiencing old ways, filter it by letting it go, and then replace
or re-frame it with a positive perspective. Remember, Mindfulness is a practice and needs to be exercised daily.
The more you practice it, the easier it will become.
-SC

Day 24

Are you tired of feeling powerless and like you're not in control? Are you ready to reclaim your power and take full accountability over your feelings and your life? It's so easy to fall off track and sometimes we end up giving people, places, and things power over us without even realizing it. If you are experiencing this or if you have ever experienced this, take a moment to complete the exercise below. After you fill it in, read it out loud three times.

1. Life got the best of me and I gave my power away to _____

Now that I am aware, I declare my power back. I recognize it is my responsibility to reclaim my power, so I will, for I am accountable. I am a deliberate being and I take my power back. I am in control. I have all that I need, everything is working out for me, and all is well.

2. Life got the best of me and I gave my power away to _____

Now that I am aware, I declare my power back. I recognize it is my responsibility to reclaim my power, so I will, for I am accountable. I am a deliberate being and I take my power back. I am in control. I have all that I need, everything is working out for me, and all is well.

3. Life got the best of me and I gave my power away to _____

Now that I am aware, I declare my power back. I recognize it is my responsibility to reclaim my power, so I will, for I am accountable. I am a deliberate being and I take my power back. I am in control. I have all that I need, everything is working out for me, and all is well.

It's easy to feel like you lost your power, but you never really lose it. Your power is always within you.
Don't forget that. What tends to happen is life gets messy and it's easy to fall off track.
When this happens, there is no need to be hard on yourself. Refocus and get back on track, do it Mindfully.
- SC

Day 25

Boundaries are key to maintaining a Mindful life. You must know what's good for you and what's not good for you. This also includes what's acceptable to you and what's not acceptable to you. You must also be comfortable with drawing your own line. Nothing or no one deserves to steal your happiness or peace, but that starts and ends with you. So, in this exercise, let's get clear on your boundaries.

1. How do you define personal boundaries?

2. Is it easy or difficult for you to assert and maintain your boundaries? Why?

3. What are three boundaries you can set for yourself starting today to ensure you don't compromise your ability to live a Mindful life?

Hi Beautiful! Congratulations! At this point of the Workbook and Guide, you've done so much work on yourself and you have completed the section on Accountability. How amazing does it feel to have reclaimed your power and let go of all that wasn't serving you? You have given yourself permission to do what makes you feel good and you have become more confident in asserting boundaries. Now, let's begin the fourth part of The Magic Four: Action.

You deserve what you tolerate and by knowing that, I hope you always have the courage
to maintain your boundaries even if it means to risk looking like a fool or disappointing someone.
- SC ·

1

2

3

Day 26 Action

This section includes questions 26-30. Please remember, the questions have been designed to introduce you to ways to implement action. These questions are not the only ways to get into action, but rather a guide to help you get started.

Healthy routines are really important because they allow you to create healthy habits. The more you do something, it becomes a habit and before you know it, you're doing it without having to remind yourself. The most important part of having healthy routines is to help keep you aligned with your goals. It also helps you reach your highest potential. In this exercise, you are invited to write out what your morning routine will include. Afternoon and evening routines are equally as important, but let's begin with creating your morning routine. This can include exercise, eating a healthy breakfast, praying, or meditating. Identify three things you will begin doing every morning starting today:

1. _____

2. _____

3. _____

Starting the morning with a routine that makes you feel good is the key to experiencing a day that feels good.
You deserve to feel good, so do things to increase your own goodness.
- SC

Day 27

In this exercise, I really want you to take some time and think about what it means to be Mindful. If you need to, please return to the beginning of this Workbook and Guide, where Mindfulness was defined and you were provided with the attitudes of Mindfulness. Knowing what you know this far about Mindfulness, how do you believe living a Mindful life can benefit you?

Identify three benefits:

1. _____

2. _____

3. _____

Now, identify three ways you intend to start practicing Mindfulness:

1. _____

2. _____

3. _____

If you believe practicing Mindfulness will be hard, you're right.
And, if you believe practicing Mindfulness will be easy, you're right. Pick the right you want to believe.
- SC

Day 28

Have you ever heard or been told that you are a vibration that creates a frequency? If you haven't and you're wondering what I mean, here it is: your vibration is the energy you give off and this is a direct reflection of your thoughts, feelings, and beliefs. If you want your experiences to be pleasant then you must do things that increase your vibration.

If you are staying in a place of anxiety, disappointment, fear, guilt, or stress it isn't possible to attract and manifest the things you desire, including pleasant experiences. This is simply because the things you desire are opposite of the unpleasant feelings. They don't match or align.

In fact, staying in a low vibration such as that of anxiety, etc., will only keep you in the cycle of repeating the same behaviors and experiences. Whereas, when you raise your vibration by thinking positive, feeling positive, and focusing on the positive, you will easily begin to attract and manifest your desires because they now match and align. Does this make sense? In other words, you can't expect high outcomes when you're vibing at a low level, but you absolutely can expect high outcomes when you're vibing high.

In this exercise, you are invited to select at least five things you can do to raise your vibration.
Please refer to the list below and feel free to add to the list:

- Begin the day with affirmations
- Exercise and eat healthy meals
- Dance. It's good for the soul
- Say no to someone or something that drains your energy
- Hang around like-minded women
- Filter negative thoughts
- Do your best not to judge your feelings and/or experiences
- Celebrate just because
- Pay it forward
- Get dressed up and take yourself out to dinner

There will be days when you wake up feeling ready to conquer the world and there will be days you feel tired and drained. It's normal. Always honor how you feel and remember you are the one, the only one, who can change the way you feel and the direction of your day. Don't let anyone or anything lower your vibration. When you really stop and think about the experience of life, you are on a planet rotating around a ball of fire next to a moon that moves the sea. If this doesn't put things into perspective and empower you to create the life you desire, then I don't know what will.
-SC

Day 29

What are you grateful for today? In this moment, stop and really ask yourself, "What am I grateful for?" Starting today, you are encouraged to begin and end each day with naming the people, places, and things you are grateful for. For today, make a gratitude list of at least three people, places, or things you are grateful for:

I am grateful for:

1. _____

2. _____

3. _____

4. _____

5. _____

6. _____

7. _____

8. _____

9. _____

Gratitude is one of the best medicines! Take a dose of gratitude every day and reap the benefits.
It will leave you feeling joyful and smiling.
- SC

Day 30

I'm sure you've heard the importance of living a balanced life and maybe at one point, you've even laughed about it because it might have seemed unattainable. It's only unattainable if you aren't clear on what you need to stay aligned mentally, physically, and spiritually. By being aligned it's easier to maintain balance because it allows you to function at your highest potential. Understand, everyone has their own idea of alignment and balance. It's whatever is doable and feels best for you. Use this space to list out what you will do to feed your mind, body, and spirit. Be specific.

In order to maintain balance and stay aligned mentally, physically, and spiritually I will do the following for my mind, body, and spirit. Identify two things for each part of you:

Mind   Body   Spirit

How many miles would you continue to drive your car if it were out of alignment?
Probably not many because you are aware of the possible risks. What makes you any different?
Every person needs an alignment. People, just like cars, function or "drive" better when they are aligned.
I encourage you to continue to keep yourself a priority and invest in your mind, body, and spirit so you stay aligned.
By doing so, you will experience joy, love, and so much more.
- SC

♥ ♥ ♥

Mind

_____
_____
_____
_____
_____

Body

_____
_____
_____
_____
_____

Spirit

_____
_____
_____
_____
_____

Mindful Makeover
Milestone

Congratulations Beautiful! You have experienced a Mindful Makeover! I hope you feel incredibly proud of yourself for making yourself a priority and dedicating time each day to work on The Magic Four. At this moment of the Workbook and Guide, you have achieved gaining awareness, accepting what is, taking accountability for your part, and you are implementing action.

You know how to filter negative thoughts and replace them with positive ones. You have a better understanding of who you are and you have identified the barriers that have kept you from living in the present moment and creating the life you desire. You have taken accountability for your behaviors and you recognize that you are responsible for creating whatever it is you want for yourself. You also recognize that you are responsible for how you respond to your feelings. You have even started taking steps of action, specifically to stay aligned mentally, physically, and spiritually. You are doing all of this and so much more!

Through this 30-day journey, you have learned how to live Mindfully, be a deliberate thinker, and stay aligned with your true essence and most authentic self. Take a moment to celebrate the work you've done thus far. You so deserve to celebrate you!

Now, it's time to create a plan to maintain Mindfulness. Completing The Magic Four was essential, but it is equally important to have a plan that will allow you to maintain this makeover. Consistency is key. Remember, it is okay to come back to this Workbook and Guide as many times as you need. Life gets busy and sometimes we end up back on "auto-pilot." However, you now have the knowledge, skills, and understanding to reclaim your POWER at any time. In the next section, you will be provided with the essentials of ways to maintain Mindfulness.

♥ ♥ ♥

Maintaining Mindfulness

Remember earlier in this guide, it was mentioned that Mindfulness is an activity and it needs to be practiced daily so it can become a "state of mind?" The intention of this Workbook and Guide was to lead you to the place where you feel confident and have the skills to begin living Mindfully, being a deliberate thinker, and staying aligned with your true essence and most authentic self.

More often than not, one's ability to stay Mindful is because their experience is hijacked by their interpretation or perception of the experience. When this happens, the person is no longer actually experiencing the experience. Also, keeping in mind interpretation or perception is just that, it's not the actual experience. To live a Mindful life is about living life in the moment without passing judgment on the experience itself. It is so easy to create a story based on past experiences and old attitudes you may have about yourself and others, but remember now you are aware and you have the skills to create healthier, more adaptive thoughts. And by doing so, this will help you live a Mindful life fueled by thoughts that will help you create the life you desire. Simply because thoughts manifest into our desires.

There are many reasons people interpret or project their perception on experiences. Sometimes, it's simply for the need to be in control, to avoid a situation that might be perceived as painful so the person jumps to conclusion to avoid having to feel unpleasant, and/or to get what the person wants. Regardless of why, this is the primary reason people aren't able to truly experience life as it's happening. The way to maintain Mindfulness is to remember and implement all the work you completed through The Magic Four and to make it a goal to create new ways for responding Mindfully rather than reacting unskillfully or as a "conditioned responder" learned from past experiences.

There are so many ways to maintain Mindfulness, but the most important is to continue to cultivate awareness and let go of any and all judgment. Remember to be Mindful that the practice of Mindfulness is a journey. It takes time to truly achieve this practice and even when you think you have achieved it, you will face challenges. This is a part of life. Allow yourself to experience life as it's happening and remember the power that lives inside of you. You are worthy and deserving of experiencing life to the fullest and it all starts with you.

- SC

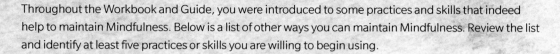

Throughout the Workbook and Guide, you were introduced to some practices and skills that indeed help to maintain Mindfulness. Below is a list of other ways you can maintain Mindfulness. Review the list and identify at least five practices or skills you are willing to begin using.

❦ *Make Mindfulness a value* ❦ *Create routines and be consistent with them* ❦ *Continue to expand and further work on Awareness, Acceptance, Accountability, and Action* ❦ *Mindfulness is truly about integrating awareness into everything we do in our lives* ❦ *Pray. Ask for what you need* ❦ *Meditate daily. It is through meditation answers are given and received* ❦ *Start every morning with an intention* ❦ *Practice gratitude* ❦ *Practice self-care* ❦ *Use positive self-talk and affirmations* ❦ *Set weekly goals and attainable tasks to achieve them* ❦ *Exercise daily, even if it's for 20 minutes* ❦ *Eat Mindfully. Your body is your temple, not a garbage disposal* ❦*

❦ *Create healthy thoughts* ❦ *Speak your desires out loud to the universe* ❦ *Take responsibility for how you want to feel* ❦ *Let go* ❦ *Forgive yourself and others. This sets you free* ❦ *Maintain awareness between your experiences versus your interpretation or perception of your experiences* ❦ *Practice being Mindful moment to moment* ❦ *Avoid judging your experiences and when you find yourself doing so, just stop and observe what you're doing* ❦ *Be inspirational and find inspiration* ❦ *Celebrate every day, for no specific reason* ❦ *Disconnect from social media* ❦ *Journal* ❦ *Watch the sunrise and set* ❦ *Go to a crystal store and purchase the crystals that resonate with you* ❦*

1._____

2._____

3._____

4._____

5._____

Bonus Exercise

Now, as we come to the end of this 30-day journey, I am inviting you to complete one last bonus exercise. In this exercise, you will begin to visualize a black canvas. You are the artist. Begin to create a visual piece / board of how you see yourself living life after experiencing a Mindful Makeover. The purpose is to create a visual and expressive reflection of the new and improved you.

Get Creative.

Use paint! Use cut outs from magazines! Color! Draw! Write! Do whatever you want. The purpose is to visualize the new and improved you and what you look like. Maybe you're strolling through a field of sunflowers, maybe you're on the beach meditating, maybe you're dancing and having fun, maybe you're enjoying time with your family. Whatever your desire is, start visualizing it, then begin creating it simply by using your imagination. Trust me - it will manifest into physical form. You deserve to create the life you desire and I believe in you!

Visual Piece / Vision Board

Use the space below and the next few pages
to create your vision.

Hi Beautiful,

As your 30-day journey through this Workbook and Guide has ended, I want to remind you that your Mindful Makeover journey is just beginning and you will experience the rewards in every moment. My wish for you is that you continue to see your potential and remember that your power lives inside of you.

You are so beautiful and powerful, so much so that you have the ability to create your own reality and truly the life you desire. Every moment has meaning and opportunity will be in every direction you choose to see it. No matter what stage of your life you're in, it's never too late or never too soon because all we have is now. I invite you to let go of living in the space of "what should have been" and live for what is happening right now in this moment. Even as you read this note, embrace whatever you feel. Soak it all in.

Please stop putting so much pressure on yourself and please stop getting in the way of your own dreams. Remember, every result you experience is your own result caused by you and how empowering to know you can change and create new results for yourself at any time. Don't worry about having all the skills to maintain this makeover. It's more about your will. Your willpower to not give up. Your willpower to face whatever life throws at you and still be able to face the day knowing you are deserving, you are enough, and you are worthy. Your willpower to keep yourself first and to love yourself like you've never been loved before.

I sincerely thank you for choosing Mindful Makeover as your guide. From my soul to yours, we are one, connected by energetic cords of light, love and the burning sun.

Love & Light,

Stephanie

*Learn more about Stephanie by visiting www.themindfulliving.com
and follow her on Instagram for daily inspiration at instagram.com/mindfulliving.now*

Course/Workshop Notes

70050440R00058

Made in the USA
Columbia, SC
19 August 2019